WHAT THE FUZZ?!

The Adventures of Fuzzberta & Friends, the World's Cutest Guinea Pigs

Monica Wu

Skyhorse Publishing

Visit our website at www.skyhorsepublishing.com.

10 9 8 7 6 5 4 3 2 1

Library of Congress Cataloging-in-Publication Data is available on file.

Cover design by Monica Wu
Cover photo credit: Monica Wu

Print ISBN: 978-1-5107-3684-9
Ebook ISBN: 978-1-5107-3686-3

Printed in China

To..........................

From.....................

Oh hello.
Fuzzberta and her furriends are
going on some grand adventures.

Won't you come along?

Donut worry, be happy.

(MiniGuineaPig says hi.)

My log has a message fur you...

(Jennifuzz's log says hi.)

Rub a dub dub,
three cubs in a tub.

(Shnoopy, Billy Blob, and Jelly Baby salute you.)

This Batman is too smol.

Wonder Woman is
quite robust though.

Cartman also seems
more robust than usual.

Let's get fuzzical!

(Fuzzberta always skips leg day.)

Treat yo' self.

Just keep swimming.

(You can keep nomming too.)

Fur sure, dude.

OH MY GLOB, YOU GUYS!

All the round things are
having a party!

Aren't you a little young to be drinking, Fuzzberta?

Fuzz and Loathing
in Blob Vegas

The Good, the Bad, and the Fuzzy

Q: Which course does
   Professor Berta teach?

A: Intro to Fuzz-ics!

Actual photo of
**George Washington
founding America.**

Fuzzlock Holmes
has a Case of the Donut Lips.

Yer a wizard, Harry!
And also a guinea pig.

The Pawmaid's Tale

(Blessed be the fuzz.)

Fuzzy I am.

From Fuzzia with Love

Is it just me, or does the Sphinx
look extra round today?

"Her life amongst the intellectuals of postwar Paris would later inspire her memoir, *A Moveable Fuzz.*"

The Rather Small Gatsby
by F. Scott Fuzzgerald

The Royal Tenenblobs

Boldly going where no fuzz
has gone before.

Q: What's a pirate's favorite food?

A: C-AARRRRR-ots!

Little Red Riding Fuzz, those
treats were for Grandma!

SHAME!! SHAME!!!

You know fuzzing,
Jon Snow.

SO HANGRY!

Fuzz of the North

brings you provisions.

You ever get the
feeling your ice cream is
smiling at you?

How does Blorpy Claus even
fit down that chimney?

We'll never know.

Q: What's Fuzzberta's favorite pancake topping?

A: More pancakes!

O Fuzzer,
where art thou?

What is Fuzzberta listening to?

Piggy Stardust,
of course.

Fun Fact:
Fuzzberta played the guitar solo
on "Bohemian Rhapsody."

Shnoop Dogg
chubbyizzle fuzzizzle

Neener! Neener!
Your meatball is mocking you!

Practice makes perfect!

(Even for guinea pigs, apparently.)

Always be yourself.

(Unless you can be a dinosaur.)

That's all, folks.
See you again soon!